WO 11/15

NSPO 2/15

Please return/renew this item by the last date shown
on this label, or on your self-service receipt.

To renew this item, visit **www.librarieswest.org.uk**
or contact your library.

Your Borrower Number and PIN are required.

History in Living Memory

Education
Through the Years

How going to school
has changed in
living memory

Clare Lewis

raintree

a Capstone company — publishers for children

Raintree is an imprint of Capstone Global Library Limited, a company incorporated in England and Wales having its registered office at 7 Pilgrim Street, London, EC4V 6LB – Registered company number: 6695582

www.raintree.co.uk
myorders@raintree.co.uk

Edited by Clare Lewis and Holly Beaumont
Designed by Philippa Jenkins
Picture research by Tracy Cummins
Production by Victoria Fitzgerald
Originated by Capstone Global Library Ltd
Printed and bound in China by Leo Paper Group

ISBN 978 1 406 29015 8
18 17 16 15 14
10 9 8 7 6 5 4 3 2 1

British Library Cataloguing in Publication Data
A full catalogue record for this book is available from the British Library.

Acknowledgements
We would like to thank the following for permission to reproduce photographs: Alamy: © Trinity Mirror/Mirrorpix, 15; Capstone Press: Philippa Jenkins, 1 Bottom Left, 1 Top Left; Corbis: © Bettmann, 14, © ClassicStock, 6; Getty Images: Bert Hardy, 7, Duane Howell/The Denver Post, 17, George Marks/Retrofile, 9, H. Armstrong Roberts, 8, Jacobsen/Three Lions, 11, Lambert, 10, Popperfoto, 13, T. Lanza/National Geographic, 16, Walter Sanders/Time Life Pictures, 12; Library of Congress: Lewis Wickes Hine, 4; Shutterstock: Carlos andre Santos, 23 Bottom, DJTaylor, 23 Middle, Everett Collection, Cover Top, Flas100, Design Element, Kolett, 23 Top, KUCO, 5 Top, Monkey Business Images, 20, 21, 22 Bottom, 22 Top Right, Pressmaster, 22 Top Left, Studio DMM Photography, Designs & Art, Design Element; SuperStock: Blend Images, Cover Bottom; Thinkstock: Big Cheese Photo, 18, Back Cover, Stockbyte, 19.

Every effort has been made to contact copyright holders of material reproduced in this book. Any omissions will be rectified in subsequent printings if notice is given to the publisher.

All the internet addresses (URLs) given in this book were valid at the time of going to press. However, due to the dynamic nature of the internet, some addresses may have changed, or sites may have changed or ceased to exist since publication. While the author and publisher regret any inconvenience this may cause readers, no responsibility for any such changes can be accepted by either the author or the publisher.

Some words are shown in bold, **like this**. You can find them in the glossary on page 23.

Contents

What is history in living memory?

Some history happened a very long time ago. Nobody alive now lived through it.

Some history did not happen so long ago.
Our parents, grandparents and adult
friends can tell us how life used to be.
We call this history in living memory.

How have schools changed in living memory?

When your grandparents were young, classrooms were not as bright and colourful as they are now.

Teachers were often very **strict** in the
old days. Children had to work quietly
and not talk to each other.

How did your grandparents get to school?

Getting to school was different from today. Not so many people had cars.

Most children walked or rode bikes to school. Children usually walked with their friends, not their parents.

How were classrooms different in the 1950s?

In the 1950s, children sat at desks arranged in rows. The teacher usually stayed at the front of the classroom.

The teacher wrote on a **blackboard** in chalk. Children copied information down on to paper.

How were lessons different in the 1950s and 1960s?

When your grandparents were young, there were no computers. Children learnt new ideas from books and from their teachers.

Girls and boys sometimes had different lessons. Some girls learnt sewing at school, while boys learnt **woodwork**.

How did children learn about the world?

Like today, pupils in the 1970s learnt about other countries. They could watch television programmes about them at school.

Some children had pen pals from around the world. They wrote letters to them to ask about life in their country.

What was school like in the 1980s?

Children sat in groups and worked together, instead of only listening to the teacher. The teacher moved around the classroom more, like today.

Computers started to be used in schools in the 1980s. Instead of writing only on paper, some children could now do their work on computers and print it out.

What changed in the 1990s?

Many teachers started to use whiteboards in the 1990s. They are brighter than blackboards and less messy.

In the 1990s, children began to use the internet at school. They could get information from people all over the world.

What is your school like today?

How do you learn at school today? Do you work alone or in groups with your classmates? Is your classroom fun and lively?

You can still learn a lot from books. Your teacher still helps you find things out. Now you can use interactive whiteboards and tablets at school, too.

Picture quiz

Which of these was used in classrooms in the 1950s?

blackboard

interactive whiteboard

tablet

How is this different from the things you use today?

Picture glossary

blackboard
dark board for writing on with chalk

strict
if someone is strict they make sure that rules are obeyed

woodwork
making things out of wood

Find out more

Books

A Photographic View of Schools (The Past in Pictures), Alex Woolf (Wayland, 2013)

History Around You (History at Home), Nick Hunter (Raintree, 2014)

Website

www.bbc.co.uk/schoolradio/subjects/history/britainsince1930s

Listen to audio clips about life in the past.

Index